MW01013562

Family Comfort Favorites
by Kim Warren

Create your own comfort food dishes by following Kim's
step-by-step easy instructions.

Photography, Steve Smith - Smith Productions - Design, Dick Brown -ThomasArts Marketing Communications

INTRODUCTION

I have been around food longer than I can remember and I've taken more cooking classes than I can count. I've been to intense week-long cooking seminars, cooking and baking classes, and worked in restaurants since I was 16. With my mom's help in the kitchen, I paid for a semester abroad in college by baking and selling homemade chocolate chip cookies. My mom is a very good cook and growing up, I always loved being in the kitchen with her. I was also inspired by my sweet grandma, Anna Pizza, who was born and spent her early years in Italy. Food is not just sustenance to Italians, it is a way of life. Food is the needle and thread that brings family and friends together. Just like I loved being in the kitchen with my mom, my own children love to be in the kitchen with me. It tickles me that they like to cook, too, and that I can share my passion for food and these special moments with them.

Some of these special moments take place with my oldest son, Charlie. He has always liked helping me in the kitchen. Charlie was born with a rare developmental syndrome called Rubenstein-Taybies syndrome. As a family we face special challenges with Charlie and in return we reap many rewards from having a child with special needs. A few years ago I became acquainted with an organization called Operation Kids and their Whole Child concept of helping kids. I was touched to learn that kids with intellectual disabilities were included in their "community" of issues and that Best Buddies was an approved and benefited charity. Best Buddies provides mentoring for teens and adults with mental disabilities. It is a wonderful organization that works with individuals near and dear to my heart. With the help of Operation Kids, it is a group that I am proud to donate a portion of each cook book sold.

I love to share my passion for cooking and my recipes with others. That is why I set out to write this book. I am inspired by women in my cooking classes who tell me they've tried a recipe at home and it was a hit with their family. One neighbor told me she made the Roasted Corn Chowder after we made it at a cooking class and she gave the recipe to her friend who made it and shared it with her extended family. Then there's my friend Lois Banks, who told me she has parents of children in the day care she runs who've asked for the Buttermilk Spice Muffin recipe because their little kids have raved about them when she has made them. Stories like these go on and on. I never dreamed I would receive the outpouring of support from so many people. That people like my food and share it with their family and friends is the best compliment I can imagine.

I am a busy mom with four very active kids. I don't have all day to cook dinner, but that doesn't mean there's only time for take-out or grilled cheese sandwiches and canned soup. My style of cooking is not fancy schmancy – I'm not gourmet and I don't know many kids that are either. But I guarantee it is great food! Food you will want to share with your loved ones. My style of cooking is what I call Family Comfort Food. The dishes in this book are just good family food that satisfies both children and adults alike. My family loves these recipes and I know your family will, too.

Soups&Sandwiches

- Asian Pork Noodle Soup
- Chicken Noodle Soup
- Chunky Sirloin Steak Chili
- Roasted Corn Chowder
- The Most Amazing Pork Roast Sandwiches
- Minestrone Soup
- Prosciutto, Tomato & Basil Panini

Asian Pork Noodle Soup

Ingredients:

1 Pork Tenderloin – fat and silver skin removed

1/2 cup Aji-Mirin (Chinese rice wine)

1/4 cup Soy Sauce

2 tsp. Dark Sesame Oil

12 cups Beef Broth

Fresh Ginger – 4 to 5 quarter-inch slices

Hard-boiled Eggs (1 per person)

Scallions – for garnish

1 package Udon Japanese Noodles or Linguini

When I was young, my mom and I would go to our local Chinese restaurant and get pork noodles. So I set out to make a soup that not only brought back those fun memories with Mom, but that also boosted the flavors from mild and subtle to bold and flavorful. This soup has accomplished both.

KIM'S NOTES: | Udon noodles take about twice as long to cook than linguini.
If your grocery store doesn't carry them, they can be found in an Asian food market.

Kim's **easy steps**

1 In a large zipper bag, combine Aji-Mirin, soy sauce and sesame oil. Add pork tenderloin and turn to coat. Zip closed, removing as much air as possible and seal tightly. Refrigerate at least 1 to 2 hours and turn 2 to 3 times during marination.

2 In a stock pot, combine beef broth and ginger slices. Bring to a low boil and add pork tenderloin but discard marinating sauce. Bring back to a boil, then reduce heat to a low simmer and poach the tenderloin for about an hour.

3 About 25 minutes before pork is done, bring a pot of salted water to a boil and cook the noodles until al dente. Drain.

4 Remove pork from the broth and let stand a few minutes, then slice into 1/4" slices against the grain.

5 In large bowls, scoop a mound of noodles in the bottom of the bowl. Top with pork slices, sliced hard-boiled eggs and a sprinkle of scallions. Then ladle warm broth over the top and serve.

This recipe is great as the **main course**.

Chicken Noodle Soup

*C*hicken Noodle Soup has got to be the ultimate comfort food. I love to whip this up on a chilly day or when someone is under the weather. Nothing says "I love you" like a big bowl of this with warm Buttermilk Spice Muffins.

Ingredients:

8 cups Chicken Broth

4 cups Water

1 to 2 Boneless, skinless Chicken Breasts

2 cups sliced Carrots (1/8" slices)

1 Tbsp. Fresh Thyme leaves

1 Shallot finely diced (or 1 small yellow onion)

1 clove Garlic, minced

Salt & pepper (white pepper preferably) to taste

Extra wide Egg Noodles

OR 2 cups Country Style dry egg noodles
(each noodle cut into fourths)

KIM'S NOTES: My favorite noodles to use in this soup are Rao's Homemade brand Fusilli. I also love Kitchen Basics Natural Chicken Stock. It is dark and very flavorful. You really can taste the difference.

Kim's **easy steps**

1 In a stock pot, combine chicken broth, water, chicken breast(s), carrots, shallot, garlic and thyme.

2 Bring to a boil, then turn down to simmer about 20 minutes or until chicken is cooked through.

3 Remove chicken from the soup to cool. Season soup with salt and pepper as necessary.

4 Bring back to a boil and add noodles. Maintain a simmer until noodles are cooked through. While noodles are cooking, dice chicken and set aside. When noodles are done, returne diced chicken to the pot. Garnish with another teaspoon or so of fresh thyme leaves and cook 2 minutes until chicken is warmed through.

5 Serve.

This recipe is great as the **main course**.

Chunky Sirloin Steak Chili

*G*rowing up, it was a tradition in my home to eat chili on Halloween. I have carried on that tradition with my chili recipe. The sirloin steak adds amazing flavor and canned beans make it quick. But please, don't think it's only for Halloween! It's great all year long. I always serve this chili with warm cornbread and honey butter.

KIM'S NOTES:

You might try garnishing with a dollop of sour cream, shredded cheddar or pepper jack cheese, Fritos, minced scallions, or all of the above. Or just eat it straight out of the pot. Either way, it's great!

Ingredients:

Olive or other light oil

1 Shallot (diced small)

3 Cloves of Garlic (finely chopped)

1 lb. Sirloin Steak cut into small chunks

1 12-oz. can Tomato Juice

1 28-oz. can Diced Tomatoes (do not drain)

2 14-oz. cans Chili Beans (do not drain)

1 14-oz. can Kidney Beans
(drained and rinsed)

1 14-oz can Red Beans (drained and rinsed)

3 Tbsp. Chili Powder (or to taste)

1 tsp. Cayenne Pepper (or to taste)

Kosher Salt

Freshly Ground Pepper

3.

5.

7.

Kim's **easy steps**

1 Over medium high heat, in a large sauce pan or dutch oven, heat enough oil to just coat the bottom of the pan. Add the shallots and garlic and sauté until they begin to sweat and lightly brown.

2 Add the steak and stir. Season with salt and freshly ground pepper. Cook until all of the juices are cooked out and the meat browns.

3 Deglaze the pan with the tomato juice and scrape the brown parts off the bottom (this makes the sauce richer). Add the diced tomatoes, and all of the beans.

4 Stir together well. Add chili powder, cayenne pepper, and salt and pepper to taste. Mix well.

5 Bring the mixture to a boil, then turn down heat and gently simmer for 30 minutes, stirring occasionally. Recheck seasonings and serve.

Roasted Corn Chowder

*I've always thought that corn chowder
tasted like creamed corn soup. I wanted
to create something with a smoky base
and lots of texture and flavor.
This soup achieves all three.
A great fall and winter soup,
but I also love to make it in the summer
when the corn is right out of the garden.*

Ingredients:

4 pieces Thick-cut Bacon,
  cut into 1/2" pieces

4 ears of Corn, husked

1 large Carrot finely diced

1 Shallot or small Yellow Onion finely diced

2 cloves Garlic minced

Loaves from 3 large sprigs of Fresh Thyme
(about 1 tsp.)

6 cups Chicken Broth

1/3 cup Wild Rice, uncooked

1/2 cup Heavy Cream

2 Tbsp. Flour

Kosher Salt

Freshly ground White Pepper

KIM'S NOTES:

The corn can be grilled or in a pinch you
can use frozen corn kernels and roast
them in the oven.

Kim's **easy steps**

1 Place ears of corn on a cookie sheet or shallow dish and roast in a 375 degree oven for 25 to 30 minutes, turning once half way through cooking time. You'll want the corn to get some brown color on it. Let cool enough to work with, then cut the kernels off the cob.

2 In the meantime, in a heavy bottomed dutch oven or stock pot, heat 1 to 2 Tbsp. of vegetable oil over medium to medium high heat and add bacon pieces. Cook the bacon, stirring often until nice and brown. With a slotted spoon, remove bacon, leaving the pan drippings behind. Then remove all but 2 Tablespoons of drippings and add carrot, shallot, and garlic;let them sauté over medium heat until they sweat, but don't brown the vegetables.

3 Add the chicken broth and scrape the sides and bottom of the pan to get the brown bits off. Bring the chicken broth to a low boil and add the corn, rice, thyme leaves and bacon. Add salt (if needed) and pepper to taste. Let simmer for 20 minutes or until wild rice is tender.

4 Whisk cream and flour together, then whisk into the soup. Bring to a simmer and let lightly bubble for 5 minutes or so until it thickens slightly and is warmed through.

5 Serve.

The Most Amazing Pot Roast Sandwiches

This dish is so incredibly easy, I'm almost embarrassed to include it in this book, but it's so yummy it just wouldn't be right to leave it out.

Ingredients:

(1) 4 to 5 lb beef brisket
(or your favorite type of pot roast),
all or most fat removed

1 can Cream of Mushroom Soup
(can be low sodium or lower fat)

1 package dry Onion Soup mix

2 tsp. granulate Beef Bouillon or
2 Beef Bouillon cubes

Freshly ground black pepper

KIM'S NOTES:

If desired, with 2 hours of cooking time left, add carrots and potatoes (such as Yukon Gold or Red Potatoes; stay away from russets - they take too long to cook), and carrots. Slice brisket in 1" thick slices and serve as a roast dinner with vegetables and gravy. Then use the leftovers for pot roast sandwiches the next day.

Kim's **easy steps**

1 Trim visible fat from pot roast and place in bottom of slow cooker. Season generously with pepper.

2 In a small bowl, whisk together remaining ingredients. Heat soup mixture in the microwave for about 30 seconds just until warm and bouillon starts to melt. Whisk again and spoon on top of pot roast.

3 Cover and cook on low 7 to 8 hours.

4 Remove pot roast from slow cooker when cooking time is complete and place in a large mixing bowl. Using two forks, shred the roast into medium or small pieces. When completely shredded, add quite a bit of the cooking gravy and mix. The mixture should be moist.

5 Place a heaping portion of pot roast on top of good bread or rolls and eat.

Ingredients:

2 Tbsp. Olive Oil

1 small Yellow Onion, finely diced

2 cloves Garlic, minced or pressed
in a garlic press

6 cups Beef Broth

1 14-oz. can Diced Tomatoes with juice

1 large or 2 medium Carrots, coarsely chopped

1 small Zucchini, chopped in ½" pieces
and quartered

1½ tsp. Sugar

1 Tbsp. Fresh Oregano, finely chopped
(or 1 tsp. dried oregano)

1¼ cup dried Small Elbow Macaroni
or small shells

2 Tbsp. Fresh Basil, finely chopped
(or 1 tsp dried basil)

2 Tbsp. Fresh Flat Leaf Parsley,
coarsely chopped

1 to 2 Tbsp. Balsamic Vinegar

Kosher Salt and freshly ground Black Pepper

Freshly grated Parmesan Cheese for garnish

Fresh Basil coarsely chopped for garnish

Kim's **easy steps**

1 In a large pot or dutch oven, heat olive oil over medium heat, add the onion and sauté about 2 minutes until it softens and becomes translucent. Add garlic and let cook about 1 minute, just until soft and aromatic. Add beef broth, tomatoes, carrot, zucchini, sugar, and oregano. Bring to a boil and reduce heat to maintain a simmer until veggies are tender but not soft, about 15 to 20 minutes. Partially cover the pot. Add macaroni and cook uncovered 10 to 12 minutes, until al dente. Stir in basil, parsley, balsamic vinegar and salt and pepper to taste.

2 Ladle into serving bowls and sprinkle with parmesan cheese and garnish with a little more fresh basil.

KIM'S NOTES:

If using dried herbs, add them when adding oregano and vegetables. Dried parsley and basil aren't as fragile as fresh, but also not as aromatic and fresh-tasting. I highly recommend fresh if at all possible.

In Italy, minestrone soup is traditionally made with beans and various leftovers. I have replaced the beans with pasta, because I love it, my kids will eat it, and it makes the soup hearty. I know there are a lot of ingredients, but it's simple to prepare.

Prosciutto, Tomato and Basil Panini

*T*his is my version of an Italian BLT. Prosciutto is an Italian ham cut paper thin. This combined with tomatoes, fresh mozzarella and basil are the key ingredients, but my secret is the balsamic vinegar. The vinegar is what really kicks the flavor into high gear and makes this sandwich amazing. I even dip the sandwich in more balsamic vinegar between bites.

Ingredients

3 slices of Prosciutto (or more if desired)

1 Tomato cut in ¼" slices; Roma tomatoes work best

Fresh Mozzarella Cheese cut into ¼" slices

4 (or so) large leaves of Fresh Basil

Balsamic Vinegar

Olive oil

2" slices bread, such as ciabatta, country sourdough, or pugliese

Kim's **easy steps**

1 Pour a couple of tablespoons of balsamic vinegar into a small bowl or ramekin. Pour a couple of tablespoons of olive oil into another small bowl or ramekin.

2 Using a pastry brush, spread some balsamic vinegar on the insides of both slices of bread. Then top one of these slices with prosciutto, followed by a couple mozzarella slices, then basil leaves, and top with tomato slices. Put second bread slice on top.

3 Brush top of sandwich with olive oil. Place oiled side down in panini machine and brush more oil on top of sandwich.

4 Lower lid and cook 3 to 4 minutes, depending on your machine, or until sandwich has pressed together and bread is golden brown.

5 Slice in half and serve.

This sandwich goes great with Hearty Minestrone Soup.

KIM'S NOTES:

This yummy sandwich can still be made without a panini press. Just heat a grill pan or a griddle to medium heat and use a heavy-bottomed pan to press sandwich down on top. When sandwich bottom is golden brown, flip sandwich over and cook until golden brown on second side.

Sides&Breads

- Garlic and Butter Sautéed Mushrooms
- Buttermilk Spice Muffins
- Glazed Carrots with Pistachio Nuts
- Creamy Parmesan Noodles
- Garlic Herb Bread
- Roasted Winter Veggies
- Gruyere and Parmesan Potato Gratin
- Grilled Corn on the Cob
- Zucchini Coins
- Sautéed Vegetable Medley with Cheddar Cheese

If you like steak sauce on your steaks, there will be no need for it with these wonderful mushrooms. The garlic butter adds amazing flavor to most of your grilled meats.

Ingredients:

2 to 4 cups assorted Mushrooms
(larger ones halved or quartered)

4 Tbsp. Butter cut into smaller cubes;
use 6 Tbsp. if doing 4 cups mushrooms

3 cloves Garlic (sliced)

Kosher Salt (preferably)

Fresh Ground Pepper

2 to 3 Tbsp. chopped Flat Leaf Parsley

Kim's **easy steps**

1 Put butter cubes and garlic slices in bottom of a small to medium saucepan. Add mushrooms and season with salt and pepper.

2 Simmer uncovered over low heat, stirring occasionally, until mushrooms are tender and most of the liquid the mushrooms will give off has cooked out. This will take about 15 minutes.

3 Add parsley and stir to combine. Serve with garlic sauce over steaks, Garlic Tri-Tip, or pork tenderloin.

KIM'S NOTES: I like to use a combination of Button, Crimini, and/or Portobello mushrooms. But feel free to try Shiitaki or any others you may like, too.

Garlic and Butter Sautéed Mushrooms

Buttermilk Spice Muffins

Ingredients

For the Muffins

1 cup Sugar

4 Tbsp. Butter, softened

1 Egg

1 cup Buttermilk

1 Tbsp. Vanilla

2 cups Flour

1 tsp. Baking Soda

1/2 tsp. Salt

For the Streusel Topping

1/4 cup Flour

1/4 cup Brown Sugar

1/4 tsp. Salt

1/2 tsp. Ground Cinnamon

Pinch of Ground Nutmeg

2 Tbsp. Butter (unsalted preferably) cold and cut into teaspoon-sized pieces

Kim's **easy steps**

These are great basic muffins that go with so much. I serve them warm with homemade raspberry jam and a bowl of soup or for breakfast with some fresh fruit.
But the best part is that kids love them!

Preheat oven to 350 degrees

The Muffins

1. In a medium mixing bowl, cream sugar and butter until smooth on medium speed with a hand beater. Add egg and vanilla and continue beating until well combined. Add buttermilk and scrape the sides of bowl with a rubber scraper. Beat until well mixed.

2. Add buttermilk and scrape the sides of bowl with a rubber scraper. Beat until well mixed.

3. In a small mixing bowl, whisk together dry ingredients and add to wet mixture. With rubber scraper, mix only until just combined. Let mixture rest in bowl while making streusel topping.

The Streusel Topping

4. In a small bowl, combine flour, brown sugar, salt, cinnamon and nutmeg. With a pastry cutter or fork, work butter into mixture until only small butter pieces remain.

5. Spoon batter evenly in a 12-cup muffin tin sprayed generously with non-stick baking spray. Top each cup of batter with a tablespoon of streusel mixture.

6. Bake at 350 degrees for 12 to 15 minutes or until a toothpick comes out clean.

What kid of any age could resist eating their carrots with a caramel sauce? For the more sophisticated palate, I threw in the pistachio nuts. Together, they hit a home run.

Kim's **easy steps**

Ingredients:

2 to 3 cups Carrots,
sliced in 1/4" diagonal pieces

3 Tbsp. packed Brown Sugar

1 Tbsp. Butter

1/3 cup Chicken Broth

Pinch of Kosher Salt

Freshly Ground Pepper

1/4 cup shelled Pistachio Nuts

2 Tbsp. finely chopped Flat Leaf Parsley

KIM'S NOTES:

When I don't have chicken broth on hand, I use chicken base that I always keep in my fridge. I substitute 1/3 cup water for the liquid.

1 Place carrots, brown sugar, butter, chicken broth, salt and pepper in a small to medium sauté pan over medium heat.

2 Bring ingredients to a simmer, stir to incorporate, and reduce to a medium low simmer for 10 minutes.

3 Add pistachio nuts and continue to cook until carrots are just fork tender.

Stir in parsley and serve immediately or cover to keep warm.

This is a quick, tasty side dish that is faster to prepare than rice and tastes like you really slaved away. It is great served with Grilled Turkey Tenderloin Medallions, Marinated Flank Steak, and Baby Back Ribs.

Ingredients:

4 cups Water
4 cups Chicken Broth
1 16-oz. box Angel Hair Pasta
2 packages dry Noodle Soup Mix
¼ cup chopped Scallions/or 1 tsp. Onion Powder
1 pint Sour Cream
1½ cub finely grated good quality Parmesan Cheese (No Green Canned!)

Kim's **easy steps**

1 Over medium high heat, bring water and chicken broth to a boil. Add dry noodle soup mix and Angel Hair pasta, (I like to break the pasta in half as I am adding it). Stirring frequently, cook until most of the cooking liquid is absorbed, but still juicy.

2 Remove from heat and stir in sour cream, scallions and parmesan cheese. Serve.

3 This recipe halves beautifully for 4 servings.

For a casserole option:
Make as above, but only add ¾ cup parmesan cheese with sour cream and scallions. Once these ingredients have been mixed well, pour mixture into a 9" x 13" dish and sprinkle top with remaining ¾ cup parmesan cheese. Bake at 350 degrees for about 25 minutes or until warmed through.

KIM'S NOTES: | This recipe can be made in advance and refrigerated until cooking time. If making in advance, add an extra 5 minutes to baking time.

Garlic Herb Bread

Crunchy on the outside, warm and soft on the inside with garlic flavor oozing from every bite. It is amazing what a few fresh herbs can do to take garlic bread to a whole new level.

Ingedients:

1 loaf of crusty Artisan Bread (such as baguette, pugliese, or ciabatta)

8 Tbsp. room temperature Butter

3 cloves minced Garlic

2 to 3 Tbsp. fresh Basil, chopped

2 to 3 Tbsp. fresh Flat Leaf Parsley, chopped

Kim's **easy steps**

Preheat oven to 375 degrees

1 Cut loaf of bread in half long ways and open up.

2 In a small mixing bowl, combine butter, garlic, basil and parsley and mix until well combined. Spread half of the mixture on each half of the bread.

3 Place bread on a baking sheet and bake 15 to 20 minutes until lightly browned. Slice and serve.

Ingredients:

2 large Beets, peeled, cut into half and then quartered

2 large Carrots, peeled and cut into 2" long pieces

2 large Parsnips, peeled and cut into 2" long pieces

1 large Sweet Yellow Onion cut into about 8 wedges

2 large Sweet Potatoes, peeled and cut into chunks roughly the same size as the beets

Extra Virgin Olive Oil

Kosher Salt

Freshly Ground Pepper

2 tsp. Fresh Thyme Leaves

Roasting is probably my favorite way to prepare vegetables. Roasting releases the sugars in the vegetables and makes them tender and sweet. Use this same process with other vegetables including asparagus and winter squashes. The biggest difference is just the cooking time.

Kim's **easy steps**

Preheat oven to 400 degrees

1 Line a baking sheet or jelly roll pan with aluminum foil. Spread prepared vegetables out on pan trying to make one layer. Drizzle olive oil generously over the top of vegetables. Season with kosher salt and freshly ground pepper and sprinkle with fresh thyme.

2 Using your hands or a rubber spatula, gently toss veggies to coat with oil and seasonings. Place baking sheet in oven and bake 40 to 60 minutes until fork tender (cooking time will vary depending on size of slices and your oven). Toss every 20 minutes during baking time to help cook evenly.

KIM'S NOTES: Feel free to experiment with the veggies in this dish. But it works best to combine veggies that have similar cooking times.

Gruyere and Parmesan Potato Gratin

This great side dish is so versatile that it can dress up your fanciest dinners like a standing prime rib, or taste like a down-home favorite when served with ham or a pork tenderloin.

Preheat oven to 375 degrees

Ingredients:

2 lbs. Yukon Gold Potatoes, peeled and cut very thin (no thicker than 1/8")

1 cup Heavy Cream

1 cup Whole Milk

2 Garlic cloves, thinly sliced

1 tsp. Fresh Thyme leaves

1½ cups grated Gruyere Cheese

¾ cup grated Parmesano-Reggiano Cheese

Kosher Salt and Freshly Ground Pepper

KIM'S NOTES:

Unfortunately this dish cannot be made in advance or the potatoes will turn black.

Kim's **easy steps**

1 Butter a 3-quart gratin or shallow baking dish. Arrange a layer of potatoes, overlapping them, season with a little salt and pepper, sprinkle with ¼ cup parmesano-reggiano cheese and ½ cup of gruyere cheese. Repeat this process with another layer, and top with a final layer of potatoes.

2 In a small saucepan, heat cream, milk, garlic, and thyme and season to taste with salt and pepper until nice and warm but not boiling. Carefully pour warm mixture evenly over potatoes. Sprinkle parmesan cheese over top followed by the final ½ cup of gruyere cheese.

3 Bake for 40 minutes or until top is golden brown and bubbly. Let stand 10 minutes to set up before serving.

Ingredients:

Grilled corn on the cob:

Fresh corn on the cob

Melted Butter

Aluminum Foil, cut in as many squares
as ears of corn.

Kim's **easy instructions**

1 Peel husks back and remove all silk strands inside, keeping husks intact. Do not cut the stems yet. Brush peeled corn with melted butter. Replace outer husks and wrap corn in aluminum foil.

2 Cook on upper rack of barbecue grill. Turn every five minutes or so. Grill should be at a temperature of about 400 degrees. Cook for a total of 15 to 20 minutes.

3 Remove foil and peel back husks. With a sharp knife, cut off husks and corn stem.

Zucchini Coins

*Z*ucchini is a garden staple that gives and gives and gives some more. I am asked often for new ways to prepare this prolific vegetable. My dad and I love our zucchini prepared like this. The corn meal gives them a lightly crunchy outside and they finish with a soft, tender center.

Kim's **easy steps**

Ingredients:

2 medium Zucchini (7 to 8" long), cut into ¼" slices

2 large or extra large Eggs

1 Tbsp. Water

¾ cup yellow Corn Meal

¾ cup all-purpose Flour

½ tsp. Kosher Salt

Olive oil or vegetable oil, for frying

KIM'S NOTES:

These little coins are great in a deep fryer if you have one. Fry in small batches. The zucchini is also great in the deep fryer when cut into spears about 4" long.

1 In dredging pans or pie pans, prepare the dipping mixtures. In the first pan, combine eggs and water and beat to combine with a whisk or fork. In the second pan, combine corn meal, flour and salt and mix well to combine.

2 Dip zucchini rounds in egg, turning to coat both sides. Transfer to corn meal mixture, coat both sides and tap to remove excess, but make sure they are well coated. Set aside on another plate. Continue this process until all zucchini rounds have been dipped and dredged.

3 In a large sauté pan over medium heat, add enough oil to generously coat bottom of pan. When oil is warm, place zucchini coins into pan in one layer. Do not over-crowd the pan. Cook a couple of minutes until bottom side gets golden brown. Using tongs, turn coins over and let brown on second side. When finished, transfer to serving plate and keep warm.

4 Add more oil to pan as necessary when cooking. Continue cooking process until all coins have been sautéed.

5 Serve.

Sautéed Vegetable Medley with Cheddar Cheese

This beautiful dish has squash, zucchini, mushrooms and tomatoes, and they are smothered in cheddar cheese. It's a great way to get kids to eat their vegetables.

Kim's **easy steps**

1 In a large sauté pan, warm olive oil over medium heat and add shallot and garlic and stir until shallots soften a bit, then add squash, stirring to coat in oil. Add tomatoes and season with salt and pepper. Cover, leaving a little crack open to let some steam escape, and let cook for 7 to 10 minutes, until tender.

2 Sprinkle cheese over the top. Cover again until cheese melts (1 to 2 minutes) and serve.

Ingredients:

2 Tbsp. Extra Virgin Olive Oil

1 large Shallot finely diced

1 clove Garlic, minced

2 medium-sized Zucchini, cut into 1" square dice

1 medium-sized Yellow Squash, cut into 1" square dice

1 cups medium-sized Button or Crimini Mushrooms, quartered

1 to 2 Roma Tomatoes diced

Kosher Salt and Freshly Ground Pepper

1 cup grated Sharp Cheddar Cheese

KIM'S NOTES:

Sharp cheddar cheese adds a lot of flavor but any kinds of cheddar cheese will do. Also, if yellow squash is not available, just use 3 zucchini instead.

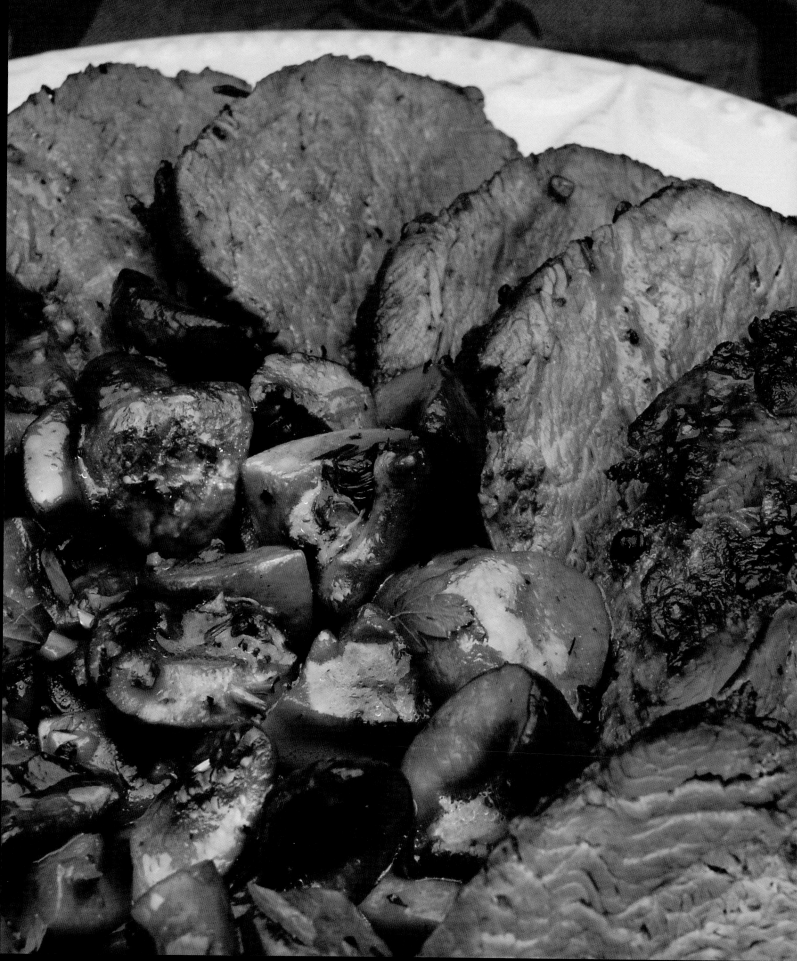

Pastas & Main Dishes

- Chicken Parmesan
- Ricotta Stuffed Shells Ricotta
- Marinara Sauce
- Grilled Turkey Tenderloin Medallions
- Homestyle Macaroni and Cheese
- Grilled Flank Steak with Asian Marinade
- Halibut with Asparagus and Potatoes
- Chicken with Macadamia Nuts
- Baby Back Ribs with Barbecue Sauce
- Italian-Style Pork Chops with Red Peppers and Mushrooms
- Pork Chops with Creamy Scalloped Potatoes
- Garlic Tri-Tip
- Grandma Annie's Meat Sauce
- Scallops in White Wine Sauce and Butter Sauce
- Linguini with Shrimp and Broccoli
- Orechiette Caprese
- Shishkabobs
- Chicken Stir-Fry
- Meatball Stroganoff

Chicken Parmesan

*Traditionally this dish is prepared with the chicken pounded thin.
I love the breasts left thick. I think it makes them more juicy, tender, and hearty.*

KIM'S NOTES: If you are in a hurry or don't want to make your own Marinara Sauce, try a jar of good Marinara. I have used Rao's and San Marzano and they are good alternatives.

Kim's **easy steps**

Ingredients:

4 to 6 Boneless, skinless Chicken Breasts, rinsed and patted dry

Olive Oil for sautéing

Chicken Coating

1/2 cup All-purpose Flour

2 Eggs, beaten

2 Tbsp. Water

1 cup plain Bread Crumbs

1 cup finely grated Parmesan Cheese

1 Tbsp. Garlic Powder

1 Tbsp. fresh Flat Leaf Parsley, finely chopped

Kosher Salt and Freshly Ground Pepper

For Baking

1 batch of Marinara Sauce (Recipe Pg. 50)

1 ball or log (about 8 oz) fresh Mozzarella Cheese, cut in 1/4" slices

1/4 to 1/2 cup grated Parmesan Cheese

1/4 cup Fresh Basil, chopped

1 In three different containers, build coating elements. In first container, add flour and season well with Kosher salt and freshly ground pepper. In second container, mix beaten eggs, water, and season with a little salt and pepper. In third container, combine bread crumbs, parmesan cheese, garlic powder, parsley, and a little black pepper.

2 One at a time, place chicken breasts in flour mixture, coating both sides, then shake off excess and place in egg mixture, coating both sides, then coat both sides in bread crumb mixture. Then set aside.

3 In a large heavy-bottomed oven-proof skillet, heat 3 to 4 Tbsp. olive oil over medium high heat until hot. Carefully add coated chicken breasts to oil and fry about 4 minutes until golden brown, then turn and sauté second side until browned.

4 Spoon Marinara Sauce over chicken breasts and place fresh mozzarella slices on top of each breast. Sprinkle with parmesan cheese and basil.

5 Place pan in oven and bake 15 to 20 minutes uncovered until cheese is melted and bubbly.

6 Serve atop a bed of boiled spaghetti.

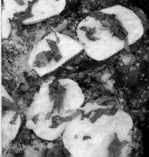

Ricotta Stuffed Shells

*T*his is a meatless main course that is hearty and delicious. Stuffing is a snap; just use a pastry bag or a gallon-sized heavy duty re-sealable bag with the corner snipped off. They are great served with a crisp green salad and Garlic Herb Bread.

KIM'S NOTES: This makes a great dish to serve at a wedding or baby shower or just for a dinner that needs to be done quick. The shells can be made in advance and refrigerated then baked just prior to serving.

Kim's **easy steps**

Ingredients:

1 box or bag Large Shells

1 large container Ricotta Cheese (approx. 4 cups)

2 eggs

1 cup shredded Mozzarella Cheese

3/4 cup grated Parmesan Cheese, divided

¼ cup fresh Flat Leaf Parsley, finely chopped

2 Tbsp. fresh Basil, finely chopped

Kosher Salt and Freshly Ground Pepper

4 oz. fresh Mozzarella, cut into ¼" slices about 1" square

4 cups Marinara sauce, see recipe on page 50, or 1 jar best quality marinara

2 Tbsp. fresh Basil, rough chopped for topping

Preheat oven to 375 degrees

1 Bring a large pot of water to a boil over high heat. Salt liberally with Kosher salt and return to a boil. Add large shells to boiling water and let cook 4 to 5 minutes, until softened a bit but not cooked through. Drain.

2 In a medium sauce pan, heat marinara sauce until it is warmed through.

3 In a mixing bowl, combine ricotta cheese, eggs, shredded mozzarella cheese, ½ cup parmesan cheese, parsley and basil. Mix with a rubber spatula or mixing spoon until well combined. Season to taste with salt and pepper.

4 Ladle half of the marinara sauce into the bottom of a baking dish. Spoon ricotta mixture into a pastry bag (or large, heavy duty re-sealable plastic bag and snip off a corner). Fill each shell with a couple tablespoons of ricotta mixture then place shell filling side up in baking dish.

5 When dish is full, ladle remaining marinara sauce over shells and place a piece of fresh mozzarella on top of each shell. Sprinkle remaining ¼ cup parmesan cheese and 2 Tbsp. basil on top of dish.

6 Cover tightly and bake 20 to 30 minutes until warmed through and fresh Mozzarella cheese softens and begins to spread.

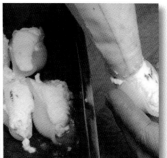

Marinara Sauce

This is a great basic sauce for pastas, Chicken Parmesan, or mixed with heavy cream for a tomato cream sauce. It tastes like it took all day to make, but it can be ready in 30 minutes or less.

Ingredients:

Olive Oil

1 large whole Shallot

3 Garlic cloves, minced

2 large (28-oz) cans of whole, peeled Tomatoes, crushed

Pinch Red Pepper Flakes

Kosher or Sea Salt and Freshly Ground Black Pepper

2 to 3 Tbsp. Flat Leaf Italian Parsley, chopped

2 to 3 Tbsp. fresh Basil, chopped

Kim's **easy steps**

1 Coat the bottom of a pan with olive oil and warm over medium heat until warm. Add shallot and let soften for a minute, then add minced garlic.

2 Cook and stir until shallots soften but don't let garlic burn, 2 to 3 minutes. Add crushed tomatoes (be careful, they can splatter) and stir. Add red pepper flakes, salt and pepper to taste.

3 Let simmer until sauce thickens, 15 to 20 minutes. Stir in basil and parsley and test sauce for seasoning. Then cover and keep warm until time to serve.

Pastas&Main Dishes

These turkey medallions and tender and plump with a delicious hint of soy. It is a great meat course for a crowd. My whole extended family prepares this for large gatherings and there are rarely any leftovers.

Ingredients:

5 lbs. Turkey tenderloins cut into large chunks, about 2" x 3" (most tenderloins will get 4 to 5 medallions)

1 12-oz. can of 7-UP

2/3 cup Soy Sauce

2/3 cup Peanut Oil

Juice of 1/2 Lemon (about 2 tablespoons)

1 large clove Garlic (minced or pressed)

1/2 tsp. raw Horseradish or 1 tsp. Horseradish Cream

Kim's **easy steps**

1 In a large bowl, whisk all ingredients together except meat until well combined. Add chunks of meat and make sure they are covered in marinade. Pour meat and marinade mixture into a large, heavy-duty resealable plastic bag. Seal bag, removing as much air as possible. Marinate in the refrigerator 5 to 6 hours or even better, overnight. Turn bag periodically to assure all meat is thoroughly coated.

2 Cook meat chunks indirectly on a 400 to 450-degree grill until they are cooked all the way through. They should get some grill marks and take on a caramel color. There should be no pink.

3 Remove meat from grill and let rest 5 to 10 minutes to redistribute juices. Serve.

KIM'S NOTES: This marinade is also great with chicken breasts. I chunk them the same as I do the turkey.
**This dish goes great with Creamy Parmesan Noodles and grilled vegetables on the side.

Homestyle Macaroni & Cheese

*T*his Mac and Cheese proves
that comfort doesn't come in a little blue box!

Ingredients:

3 Tbsp. Unsalted Butter

3 Tbsp. All-purpose Flour

6 cups grated Extra Sharp Cheddar Cheese

4 cups Whole Milk

Kosher Salt

Freshly Ground White Pepper

1 pound elbow or small Shell Macaroni

KIM'S NOTES:

I like to use Tillamook's Extra Sharp White Cheddar Cheese. It comes in a black wax coating and is available in most markets and at Costco but any sharp cheddar cheese will be good.

Kim's **easy steps**

Preheat oven to 400 degrees

1 Bring a pot of salted water to a boil over medium high heat, add macaroni and cook until 6 to 7 minutes. It will not be quite cooked, but will finish in the oven. Drain.

2 While macaroni cooks, melt butter over medium heat in a large, deep sauté pan. Whisk in flour and cook for one minute, whisking constantly so it will not burn. This mixture will turn a golden color. Continue whisking constantly; in a steady stream, add milk and cook until smooth and slightly thickened.

3 Stir in 5 cups of cheese (reserving 1 cup to sprinkle on the top). Stir until cheese is completely melted. Season to taste with additional salt and pepper.

4 Add the cooked and drained macaroni and stir to coat well.

5 Pour this entire mixture into a 9" x 9" (or similar size) casserole dish and sprinkle remaining cheese evenly over top.

6 Bake uncovered for 30 minutes until bubbly and golden brown on top.

This recipe is great as a **main course** or a hearty **side dish**.

My friend Merilee Walker gave me a recipe her family uses for flank steak. I tried it and thought it was great, but I always like to put my own spin on things. I kicked up the Asian element by changing and adding a few ingredients. I think this is a nice adaptation of their recipe.

Ingredients:

1 Flank Steak, trimmed, visible fat removed

Gallon-sized resealable plastic bag

1 Recipe Asian Marinade (see below)

Asian Style Marinade

¾ cup Peanut Oil

¼ cup Soy Sauce

¼ cup Honey

2 Tbsp. Rice Wine Vinegar

2 Tbsp. Scallions, finely chopped

2 cloves Garlic, minced

1 Tbsp. Fresh Ginger, peeled and minced

This marinade is also good with sirloin steak for kabobs or on chicken instead of teriyaki.

Kim's **easy steps**

In a medium bowl, combine all ingredients and whisk together until well blended. Make sure honey is well combined. Pour over meat in a resealable heavy duty bag. Refrigerate 5 to 6 hours or overnight.

1 Place flank steak in the resealable plastic bag. Pour marinade over steak and seal bag tightly. Refrigerate and let marinate 5 to 6 hours or better yet, overnight.

2 Remove from grill and let rest 5 to 10 minutes.

3 Slice thin (about 1/8" slices) on a sharp angle against the grain of the meat and serve.

KIM'S NOTES: Do not overcook this cut of meat. It can get tough. Flank steak is best cooked to no more than medium temperature

Grilled Flank Steak
with Asian Marinade

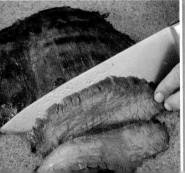

Kim's **easy steps**

1 With a pastry brush, brush a light coat of olive oil in the middle section of a piece of foil.

2 Place a halibut piece in the center of the foil piece.

3 Place 2 or 3 asparagus spears on the top side and bottom side of the halibut.

4 Place a handful of potato chunks on the right and left sides of the halibut.

5 Dab a little olive oil on top of the fish, asparagus and potatoes.

6 Season everything with some salt and pepper.

7 Place a sprig of thyme on top of fish and remove leaves from a second sprig of thyme and sprinkle leaves on top of potatoes and asparagus.

8 Wrap up by bringing long sides of foil together then roll down until it meets the ingredients inside. Then fold sides in as if wrapping a present. Be careful not to puncture foil. If foil rips or gets a hole, wrap in a second piece or food won't cook well.

9 Place on a hot grill (375 to 400 degrees) and let cook 6 minutes. Turn with tongs and cook 6 minutes on other side.

10 Check a pouch. Fish should be white and moist, but should not be pink or raw in the middle. If still raw-looking, wrap back up and return to grill for a couple more minutes.

11 Serve with a couple slices of lemon.

Ingredients:

¼ cup Extra Virgin Olive Oil

1½ to 2 lbs. fresh Halibut fillet, cut into 6 - to 8 - oz. piece

1 bundle medium sized Asparagus, washed and trimme

3 to 4 large Yukon Gold Potatoes, scrubbed and cut into ½" diced chunks

8 to 10 fresh Thyme sprigs

Kosher or Sea Salt

Freshly Ground White Pepper

1 Lemon cut into 8 wedges

Aluminum Foil cut into 14" long rectangular pieces

KIM'S NOTES: I was taught by Rob, the owner of the Cooking School of Aspen, that when buying fresh fish, smell it. If it smells fishy, don't buy it. The fishy smell means it is old. This advice has worked for me. Thanks, Rob! My daughters love to build these fish pouches. We like to build them differently for each member of the family. Some like more asparagus than others, etc. Then we put the first letter of each person's name with permanent marker on each foil pouch so we know whose is whose. Take this to your next "Bring Your Own Meat" barbecue and be the envy of your friends.

Halibut with Asparagus and Potatoes

*T*his is an absolutely beautiful dish that will make you feel like a Boy Scout when you prepare it.
All of the ingredients are wrapped into a foil pouch and grilled to perfection in 12 minutes.

The best news is that your house won't smell like fish, but you get to enjoy Halibut prepared to perfection!

Kim's **easy steps**

*T*his chicken dish is divine! I crave it often and get a rousing approval from the troops when I make it. My mom made it when I was growing up, but used cashews instead of macadamia nuts; it is tasty that way, too. Either way, I know you'll thank me when you try this one.

Ingredients:

For the chicken

4 Boneless, Skinless Chicken Breasts, rinsed and patted dry

½ cup Corn Starch

1 tsp. Kosher Salt

1 quart-sized resealable bag

About ½ cup Vegetable Oil, for frying

For the sauce

6 Tbsp. Soy Sauce

4 Tbsp. Dry Sherry

2 Tbsp. Granulated Sugar

3 cups Chicken Stock

1¼ cups dry roasted Macadamia Nuts

1 Cut chicken breasts into chucks about 1" wide and 2 to 3" long (each breast should make 4 to 5 pieces). Put cornstarch and salt into resealable bag and shake well to mix. Add about 5 chicken pieces and shake to coat; set aside on a plate and repeat process until all chicken has been dredged.

2 Heat a large sauté pan over medium to medium high heat and add vegetable oil. Oil should be about 1/8" deep in the bottom of the pan. Sauté dredged chicken until golden brown on both sides. Do not overcrowd pan. It is better to do two batches than try to jam all of the chicken in one pan. If chicken pieces touch they will steam making it difficult to brown and make crisp.

3 While chicken is browning, combine all sauce ingredients except for macadamia nuts in a medium mixing bowl and whisk together to mix well.

4 When all chicken has browned, pour off any excess oil in pan. Return all chicken pieces to pan and pour sauce over chicken. Bring to a boil, then cover, leaving only a small venting hole for steam to escape, reduce heat to maintain a low simmer. Let cook 60 to 90 minutes until chicken is tender, stirring occasionally.

5 Ten minutes before serving, check to see that sauce has thickened, then add macadamia nuts and stir to coat in sauce. If sauce is still thin, make a little slurry with ¼ cup chicken broth or water and a heaping tablespoon of cornstarch. Stir in before adding nuts. Once mixed in, add nuts and let cook about 10 minutes longer.

6 Serve with steamed sticky rice and broccoli or asparagus on the side.

KIM'S NOTES: The secret to this dish is to give it the full 60 to 90 minutes of simmering time. The chicken gets so tender that it cuts easily with a fork.

Chicken with Macadamia Nuts

Baby Back Ribs with Barbecue Sauce

These ribs are so good that they are a regular request from my family, particularly the men. It is a tradition to serve these on Super Bowl Sunday and at summer barbecues. Braising makes these ribs tender but store-bought barbecue sauce is my shortcut secret. My favorite sauce is Tony Roma's Original.

Ingredients:

2 Racks Baby Back Ribs

Kosher or Sea Salt

Freshly ground Black Pepper

1 container of your favorite barbecue sauce

KIM'S NOTES:

Try making the Garlic Herb Bread on the grill. It can cook along with the ribs and corn. This way, you don't have to heat the oven back up. Put bread halves back together and wrap in a double layer of foil. Cook on upper rack of grill. Turn bread over halfway through cooking time.

Kim's **easy steps**

Preheat oven to 325 degrees

1 Season ribs liberally with salt and pepper. Place ribs bone side down in a 9x13x2" (or larger) baking dish. Add about ½" of water to dish. Be careful not to cover ribs with water or they will stew.

2 Cover baking dish tightly with a double layer of foil. If not sealed tightly the water will evaporate and ribs could burn. Bake for 2½ hours. Check water level a couple of times. If water is getting low, add more water to dish and reseal foil.

3 Remove ribs from oven and baking dish. Ribs can be grilled right away or refrigerated to finish later. When ready to serve, grill over medium heat, meaty side down. Using a large pastry brush, spread barbecue sauce liberally on bony side of ribs. Grill until the meaty side of ribs browns, 3 to 4 minutes. Turn over and baste meaty side of ribs with sauce. After 3 to 4 minutes, when bony side is getting brown and crispy, remove ribs from grill and place on a platter.

4 I like to cut these into 3 to 4 rib slabs and serve family style.

These ribs go great with Creamy Parmesan Noodles and Garlic Herb Bread, and Grilled Corn on the Cob.

Italian-Style Pork Chops with Red Peppers and Mushrooms

This dish is my dad's very favorite! It came from my Aunt Marie. I have converted it to the slow cooker and added a few twists of my own.

Ingredients:

4 to 6 thick cut bone-in Pork Loin Chops

14-oz. can Tomato Sauce

1 clove Fresh Garlic, minced

1½ tsp. fresh or ½ tsp. dry Oregano

1 Red Bell Pepper

1 Yellow or Orange Bell Pepper

8 to 12 large Button or Crimini Mushrooms

Mozzarella Cheese (preferably fresh)

Garlic powder

Onion powder

Kosher Salt and Freshly Ground Pepper

Kim's **easy steps**

1 Generously season pork chops on both sides with garlic powder, onion powder, salt and pepper. Grill, broil, or pan fry until nicely browned on both sides. Then place in the bottom of slow cooker and top with any remaining pan juices.

2 In a small bowl mix tomato sauce, garlic, oregano and a pinch of pepper. Pour over top of pork chops and cover slow cooker. Cook for 7 to 8 hours on low.

3 Seed the peppers and cut into 6 to 8 slices. Clean and stem mushrooms. With 1 to 2 hours of cooking time remaining add peppers and mushrooms to slow cooker.

4 Slice fresh mozzarella into ¼" pieces (or if using pizza-type mozzarella it can be grated). 5 to 10 minutes prior to serving, top each pork chop with mozzarella. Turn slow cooker to high and cover. Cook just until mozzarella is melted.

5 **To serve:** Top each pork chop with a pepper slice and mushroom and spoon sauce on top. You may want to pour remaining sauce into a bowl and pass at the table.

KIM'S NOTES:

This dish is great served with Creamy Parmesan Noodles, a seasoned rice or atop warm soft polenta.

Pork Chops with Creamy Scalloped Potatoes

*P*ork chops are my favorite things to make in the slow cooker because they are usually very dry when cooked using other methods. The slow cooker makes pork chops moist and tender. I also like to use cuts with the bone because the bones help to keep them moist. Taking the extra couple of minutes to brown the pork chops adds wonderful flavor to the meat.

Ingredients:

4 to 6" thick cut bone-in Pork Loin Chops

Onion Powder

Garlic Powder

Salt and Freshly Ground Pepper

4 to 6 large Yukon Gold or Russet potatoes, peeled and cut into ¼" slices

1 can Cream of Mushroom Soup

1 cup Sour Cream

2 Tbsp. Flat Leaf Parsley

Kosher Salt and Freshly Ground Pepper

KIM'S NOTES: | I often season and grill the pork chops in advance and refrigerate overnight. The rest of the dinner will assemble in just a few minutes the next day.

Kim's **easy steps**

1 Generously season both sides of pork chops with onion powder, garlic powder, salt and pepper. Then grill, broil, or pan fry just until nicely browned on both sides and set aside.

2 Spray slow cooker with cooking spray and place a layer of potatoes on the bottom (the potatoes can overlap a little). Season potatoes with salt and pepper, then carefully cover with ¼ of soup mixture.

3 Repeat layering potatoes, salt and pepper and soup mixture two more times so that you have 3 layers of potatoes. Place browned pork chops on top of potatoes and cover with remaining soup mixture and any juices from resting pork chops.

4 Cover slow cooker and cook on low for 7 to 8 hours (or high for 3 to 3 ½ hours).

I have seen the tri-tip called both a roast and a steak. In this recipe, it is considered a steak. The tri-tip has excellent flavor and goes a long way. This cut is a reasonably priced way to let the whole family have steak for dinner.

Ingredients

1 Tri-tip Steak, 2 to 3 lbs.

Extra Virgin Olive Oil (about 1 Tbsp.)

5 to 6 large cloves Fresh Garlic minced or pressed in a garlic press

About 1½ tsp. Kosher or Sea Salt

About 1½ tsp. freshly ground Black Pepper

1 hour before preparing, remove meat from refrigerator and bring to room temperature.

Kim's **easy steps**

Preheat oven to 375 degrees

1 With a pastry brush (or your hands), coat meat on both sides with olive oil, then liberally season with garlic, salt and pepper.

2 Heat grill pan or large oven-proof sauté pan until very hot. If using a sauté pan, add additional olive oil to coat bottom of pan. Using tongs, carefully place meat in hot pan. Cook until the side that is down is nicely browned, then carefully turn with tongs and brown other side.

3 Place pan and meat into oven and roast 10 to 15 minutes longer, using a meat thermometer, cook until meat is 10 degrees below desired doneness. Remove from oven and transfer to cutting board and let stand 5 to 10 minutes. Meat will continue to cook while resting.

4 Cut in ½" slices against the grain and serve.

KIM'S NOTES: | These are great served with garlic and butter sautéed mushrooms.

Garlic Tri-Tip

Grandma Annie's Meat Sauce

My grandparents were full blooded Italians from the old country. This recipe was passed down to my grandma from her mother and she passed it to my mom. As far as my parents and siblings are considered, this truly is our family's comfort food. This recipe calls for beef stew meat, but grandma also made it with chicken, Italian sausage and lamb, whatever was on sale. In 2002, Grandma passed away just 2 months before her 101st birthday.

Ingredients:

Extra Virgin Olive Oil

2 to 2½ lbs. Beef Stew Meat, any big chunks of fat removed

3 cloves fresh Garlic, minced

3 to 4 28-oz cans Whole Tomatoes, (preferably San Marzano tomatoes), crushed

1/2 small can Tomato Paste

1/3 cup chopped fresh Flat Leaf Parsley

Kosher or Sea Salt

Freshly ground Black Pepper

KIM'S NOTES: Kim's notes: Grandma made this sauce with tomatoes she had bottled from her garden. She added a can of tomato paste for each quart-sized jar of bottled tomatoes because they contained so much juice. Most canned tomatoes don't contain as much juice, particularly San Marzano or plum style tomatoes. Use more tomato paste as a thickening agent, but I don't recommend adding until after a couple hours of simmering time.

Kim's **easy steps**

1 Over medium heat in a heavy-bottom large sauce pan or enamel dutch oven, heat enough olive oil to coat bottom of pan. When hot, add meat and garlic and stir. Season with a large pinch (about ½ tsp.) of salt and pepper. Brown until juices cook down and meat browns nicely on all sides. This browning creates great flavor.

2 Open 3 cans of tomatoes, reserving 4th can as needed. Pour into a large mixing bowl and crush one can at a time (this works the very best with your hands). Carefully add tomatoes to browned meat — they are notorious for spattering. Then stir in tomato paste and chopped parsley.

3 Bring mixture just to a boil, reduce heat to a low simmer and cover, leaving lid slightly ajar to allow steam to escape. Let simmer very low for several hours, stirring occasionally to keep from burning on the bottom.

4 Ladle over just-drained pasta — our favorites are rigatoni and gnocchi — and gently stir to incorporate.

5 If after a few hours of low simmering, the sauce seems extremely thick, add juice from the 4th can of tomatoes. Add tomatoes as needed.

Ingredients:

1 lb. Sea Scallops

All-purpose Flour (about ¾ cup) for dredging

5 Tbsp. Unsalted Butter, divided

1 large Shallot medium diced, about ¼ cup

1 clove Garlic, minced

½ cup dry White Wine

3 Tbsp. Flat Leaf Parsley, chopped

1 Tbsp. fresh Thyme leaves, chopped

Juice of half a Lemon

Kosher Salt and Freshly Ground Black Pepper to taste

This recipe is simple to make, but it tastes like it came from a gourmet restaurant. These scallops are great served over a little angel hair pasta or with basmati rice. Don't forget to spoon on plenty of the sauce!

Kim's **easy steps**

1 Rinse scallops and pat to dry with paper towel. Season both sides with salt and pepper, then dredge in flour and tap off any excess flour.

2 Heat 2 Tbsp. butter in a large sauté pan over medium high heat until melted and sizzling; add scallops. Don't let scallops touch each other or they will steam and not brown properly. Lower heat to medium and cook until they are golden brown on one side, 2 to 3 minutes. Using tongs, turn over and allow to brown on second side. Do not move scallops around while cooking. Remove scallops from pan and set aside.

3 With pan on medium heat, add wine and scrape with wooden spoon to deglaze and release any stuck pieces. Add remaining 3 Tbsp. butter. When butter is melted, add shallots and garlic and sauté until shallots soften. Add fresh herbs and lemon juice and cook another minute. Season to taste with salt and pepper.

4 Place scallops on serving platter or on top of pasta or rice and cover with warm sauce. Serve.

Scallops in White Wine and Butter Sauce

Ingredients:

1 lb. package dry Linguini Noodles

4 Tbsp. Unsalted Butter

4 Tbsp. Extra Virgin Olive Oil

3 cloves Garlic, minced

2 cups Broccoli, cut into little crowns

16 to 18 extra-large Shrimp, washed, deveined and shelled to the tail

½ cup Dry White Wine

Juice of ½ lemon

Kosher Salt and Freshly Ground Pepper

1 Tbsp. Flat Leaf Parsley, finely chopped

This is a hearty, quick dish. It is easy to prepare and tasty enough to serve for a dinner party. I love it served with a fresh green salad and some Garlic Herb Bread.

Kim's **easy steps**

1 Bring a large pot of generously salted water to a rolling boil. Add linguini noodles and stir to keep from sticking together. Cook until al dente.

2 In the meantime, over medium low heat, add butter and olive oil to a large sauté pan. When butter has melted, add garlic and stir, cooking until garlic becomes opaque and fragrant. About 1 minute. Turn heat up to medium, add broccoli pieces and coat in sauce. Cover and let cook about 4 minutes, stirring occasionally, until broccoli just starts to get tender (it may brown a little).

3 Add shrimp. Try not to let shrimp touch each other. Let simmer 3 minutes or until they become pink on the bottom side. Turn shrimp over and add wine and lemon juice. Season with salt and pepper and sprinkle with parsley. Cook shrimp until just pink on the second side. Add freshly drained linguini noodles directly to shrimp pan. Turn pasta with tongs to coat in butter sauce and pour into serving bowl. Garnish with more parsley.

4 Enjoy!

Orecchiette Caprese

*T*his is a fancy name for a simple dish with tomatoes, basil, and fresh mozzarella. Orecchiette means "little ear" in Italian and that's exactly what these little noodles look like. The best part is they trap sauce, cheese and tomatoes in every bite!

Ingredients:

1 lb. Orecchiette Pasta

1/3 cup Extra Virgin Olive Oil

4 cloves Garlic, minced or pressed

4 to 5 lg. Roma Tomatoes, seeded,
2 cups grape tomatoes, halved **or**
1 28-oz. can of diced tomatoes, drained

¼ cup Basil, roughly chopped

8 oz. Fresh Mozzarella, diced

Kosher or Sea Salt

Freshly ground Black Pepper

Kim's **easy steps**

1 Bring a large pot of water to a boil over high to medium high heat. When water comes to a full rolling boil, salt it generously. When a full boil returns, add pasta and stir well to keep from sticking together. Cook until al dente, about 8 minutes.

2 Heat olive oil over medium low heat in a large sauté pan. Add garlic and let cook 1 to 2 minutes until fragrant and softened. Add tomatoes and heat through, stirring often about 2 minutes. Season with salt and pepper and add basil. Remove from heat. Add drained pasta directly to sauce pan and stir to coat. Pour into serving bowl.

3 Add mozzarella and toss to combine. Season if necessary, and serve.

Ingredients:

2 lbs. Sirloin Steak 1 to 1½" thick, cut in 2" cubes

Mr. Yashida's Sauce, or your favorite teriyaki sauce

6 large Crimini or Button Mushrooms, cleaned and stems removed

1 Red Bell Pepper, seeds removed and cut in 1" wide strips

1 Yellow or Orange Bell Pepper, seeds removed and cut in 1" wide strips

1 large Purple Onion, cut into 6 or 8 wedges

6 to 8 Pineapple Chunks (1 ½" cubes), preferably fresh pineapple

6 to 8 Campari or Cherry Tomatoes

6 to 8 long metal skewers (wood skewers can be used in a pinch)

I love meat, veggies and fruit grilled, and this is the perfect way to get all three in one neat little package. My family likes kabobs because they can each customize one with their favorite ingredients.

KIM'S NOTES: This recipe is shown with chunks of sirloin steak marinated in teriyaki, but they are also great with chicken breast and/or pork tenderloin chunks, shrimp or any combination. Also, be adventurous with the veggies! I sometimes add zucchini spread with garlic butter, canned white potatoes, baby corn cobs, or any fruit or vegetable that can be skewered and grilled.

Kim's **easy steps**

1 In a gallon-sized resealable plastic bag, place sirloin steak chunks and enough teriyaki sauce to nicely coat the meat. Seal tightly and toss gently to thoroughly coat. Refrigerate for at least one hour or up to overnight.

2 If using wood skewers, soak them in a bowl or in the sink, immersed in water for an hour before assembling.

3 When ready to put skewers together, gather all elements and begin with a chunk of meat, followed by a mushroom cap, then steak again, followed by a strip of both bell peppers, then steak again, and an onion wedge and a pineapple chunk, one last piece of steak and a tomato to finish things off.

4 Repeat this process until all skewers are loaded. If there is leftover meat or vegetables, I like to make individual skewers of just meat, or just pineapple and people can have a couple more of their favorite elements.

5 When assembling skewers, be careful not to mash meat together with other elements or it may have a difficult time cooking evenly. Try to leave a little bit of space between elements so they can all cook properly.

6 Heat grill to between 375 – 400 degrees. Place assembled skewers on the grill either horizontally or vertically. Let them cook 5 or so minutes and check. Look for the bottom side to brown nicely. Use tongs or oven mitts to turn the skewers, and be careful not to let the pineapples or tomatoes fall off.

7 When meat has reached desired temperature, remove skewers from the grill and allow to rest 5 to 10 minutes before serving.

I usually serve these with steamed sticky rice and some fresh fruit or tossed green salad.

Chicken Stir-fry

This dish is super quick and super tasty! Most of the ingredients can be prepped in advance and then kept in the refrigerator. The ginger and garlic give this dish great flavor, and it's loaded with bite-sized vegetables. I usually steam some sticky rice to go with this, but it's also great over Asian-style noodles.

gredients:

Boneless, Skinless Chicken Breasts
t into ½" strips

. Yashida's sauce, or your
vorite teriyaki sauce

Tbsp. Peanut or vegetable oil

Shallot, minced

cloves Garlic, minced

cup Broccoli florets, cut into small pieces

cup Baby carrots or 1 large carrot
Jt into ½" slices

cup Asparagus spears cut into ½" slices

cup Zucchini chunks cut into approx. ½" cubes

Red Bell Pepper, seeds removed and julienned

cup Button Mushrooms,
tems removed, quartered

Tbsp. Fresh Ginger Root, minced

cup Snap Peas

cup Whole Salty Cashews

KIM'S NOTES:

his dish cooks better when vegetables are cut
nto bites approximately the same size. I have used
chicken in this version, but you could also use some
sirloin or filet mignon steak as well. Peanuts could
also be substituted for cashews if necessary.

Kim's **easy steps**

1 Place chicken breast strips in a resealable plastic bag and add about ½ teriyaki sauce (or enough to nicely coat meat). Refrigerate for at least an hour or up to overnight.

2 Remove chicken strips from teriyaki sauce, but reserve sauce for later. In a wok or large skillet, over high heat, add peanut oil.

3 When oil is hot, add chicken strips, shallot and garlic and cook, stirring constantly until chicken turns opaque on both sides.

4 Add broccoli florets, carrots, and asparagus, and stir. Let cook about a minute and add reserved teriyaki sauce stir to incorporate. Add zucchini, red pepper, mushrooms, and ginger.

5 Stir frequently to keep everything cooking evenly. Cook a couple of minutes more until zucchini begins to soften a bit and all veggies are tender crisp. Add snow peas and cashews and stir to incorporate. Let cook another minute or so, careful not to overcook. Vegetables should be tender, crisp but not crunchy.

6 Serve.

Meatball Stroganoff

When I was young my mom made this dish and we loved it. She made the meatballs from scratch, sautéed them in a frying pan, let them cool and then added them to the sauce. It was a really special meal. Now it is a favorite of my family. I have jazzed the sauce up a touch and I buy the little frozen Italian meatballs and save tons of time.

Ingredients

¼ cup All-purpose Flour

1 ¼ cup Sour Cream

1 10½-oz. can Beef Consommé soup

3 Tbsp. Tomato Paste

½ tsp. Worcestershire Sauce

1 large clove Garlic, finely minced or pressed through a garlic press

Pinch of salt

14 frozen Italian-style Meatballs

1 small can sliced Black Olives — do not drain

Kim's **easy steps**

Preheat oven to 300 degrees

1 In a medium-sized stovetop and oven-proof baking dish whisk together flour and sour cream over medium low heat until smooth and almost shiny. Stir constantly, this can burn easily.

2 Add consommé, tomato paste, Worcestershire sauce, garlic and salt. Whisk together until combined and smooth. Heat until mixture just begins to simmer.

3 Add frozen meatballs. Cover with lid or aluminum foil and bake for 1 hour.

4 With about 25 minutes left in cooking time add noodles to a generously salted pot of boiling water and cook until al dente.

5 With about 15 minutes of cook time remaining, add black olives and their juices and mix carefully. Cover again and finish cooking.

6 Serve over prepared noodles

KIM'S NOTES:

I like using Rao's Fusilli noodles for this dish but any good wide noodles will work. This is a great make-ahead dish. Prepare through step 3 and refrigerate until ready to bake. Bake at 325 degrees instead.

Cakes&Desserts

- Blackberry Cobbler
- Chocolate Cake with Almond Cream and Rasberries.

- Poppy Seed Cake with Almond Glaze

- Pizzookie

- Gwen's Cherry Cream Pie

Blackberry Cobbler

Not only is this dessert absolutely divine, it is also beautiful, with these gorgeous, plump purple berries. I can't wait until blackberries come into season to make this. It is also delicious made with mixed berries.

Ingredients:

Filling

to 8 cups fresh Blackberries, washed and
drained or 2 bags frozen blackberries
thawed and drained, reserving liquid.

2 cup Cornstarch

cup Sugar

/4 tsp. Salt

/3 cup Water (or reserved liquid
from frozen berries)

Biscuit Topper

cup All-purpose Flour

Tbsp. Sugar

1/2 tsp. Baking Powder

/4 tsp. Salt

Tbsp. Butter, cold

lightly beaten Egg

/4 cup Milk

Kim's **easy steps**

Preheat oven to 400 degrees

1 In a medium saucepan, combine cornstarch, sugar, salt and whisk together.

2 Add water; on medium high heat bring to a boil, stirring frequently.

3 As soon as it comes to a boil, reduce heat to medium and stir constantly until sauce thickens to the consistency of a glaze or syrup.

4 Place blackberries in a 9" deep dish pie pan or baker. Pour hot syrup over blackberries and gently combine to coat the berries.

Set aside while making biscuit topper.

5 In a medium mixing bowl, combine flour, sugar, baking powder and salt. Cut in cold butter with a pastry mixer or fork until only pea-sized pieces remain.

6 Add egg and milk and mix only until ingredients come together and are moistened. Don't over-mix or biscuits will be tough.

7 Spoon 6 mounds of dough over berry filling, spacing equally. Place pie pan on a baking sheet to catch any overflow spills and bake for 40 – 45 minutes until biscuits are deep golden brown and filling is bubbly.

Serve warm with vanilla ice cream.

desserts

Kim's **easy steps**

Ingredients for the Cake:

1 Devils Food Cake Mix

1/2 cup Semi-sweet Chocolate Chips

Ingredients for Almond Cream

1 1/2 cups Heavy Whipping Cream

1/4 cup (or more to taste) Powdered Sugar

1 tsp. Pure Almond Extract

For the Raspberries

4 cups firm Raspberries gently rinsed and drained thoroughly.

For the Strawberries

3 to 4 cups ripe Strawberries washed, drained and cut into 1/4" slices.

This cake is also wonderful with fresh strawberries. Use whichever is in season. Just never use frozen berries on this one!

1 Make cake according to package directions, but once mixing is done, hand stir in half of the chocolate chips and pour into liberally sprayed 12" cake pan or two 9" cake pans.

2 Sprinkle rest of chocolate chips evenly on top of batter. Bake according to package directions (use time for 13 x 9" pan as a reference for the 12" round cake pan but check earlier).

3 Let cake completely cool in pan, then invert cake flat side up to a serving platter or cardboard cake round.

For the Almond Cream

4 In a medium-sized mixing bowl, whip cream until soft peaks form. Add powdered sugar and almond extract. Beat until stiff, but be careful not to over-beat. It will get dry and start to look like whipped butter.

5 ### For the Raspberry Cake
In a thick layer, spread almond cream on top of cake. Starting from the outside edge, place raspberries in a large circle all the way around the cake, then continue working in with circles gradually getting smaller until the entire cake is covered with raspberries.

6 ### For the Strawberry Cake
Cut strawberries into 1/4" round slices. Then cover the almond cream with strawberries working in circles as with the raspberries.

KIM'S NOTES: | *Eat soon. This cake does not keep for long periods of time. If not serving immediately, refrigerate!*

Chocolate Cake with Almond Cream and Raspberries

Ingredients

For the cake

1 Yellow Cake mix

1 small package French Vanilla Instant Pudding mix
   (vanilla instant pudding is fine, too)

1 cup Sour Cream

1/2 cup Water

4 Eggs

1/2 cup Vegetable Oil

2 Tbsp. Poppy Seeds

2 Tbsp. Pure Almond Extract

For the glaze

2 cups sifted Powdered Sugar

2 Tbsp. Milk

1 - 2 tsp. Almond Extract

Kim's **easy steps**

KIM'S NOTES:

This cake is great just dusted with powdered sugar, or baked with sugar in the bottom of the pan. It can also be made in loaf pans or into muffins. Be creative!

Preheat oven to 350 degrees

For the Cake

1 Combine all ingredients in a mixing bowl and beat on medium speed for 3 minutes.

2 Liberally spray a bundt pan with pan release or cooking spray and set aside.

3 Scrape down sides of bowl and combine with a spoon and pour batter in prepared cake pan.

4 Bake at 350 degrees for 40 to 50 minutes, until a cake tester or toothpick comes out clean. Remove to cooling rack and let rest for 15 minutes. Then remove cake onto serving plate and let cool completely.

For the Glaze

5 Whisk powdered sugar and milk together well until smooth and of pouring consistency. Add 1 tsp. almond extract and mix well.

6 If glaze is too thick, thin using small amounts of milk until correct consistency is achieved. Taste and add more almond extract if needed for flavor.

7 Glaze cake by slowly pouring glaze over the middle of the cake and letting the glaze drip down the sides of the cake.

Poppy Seed Cake with Almond Glaze

This cake couldn't be easier! Everything dumps into one bowl, is beaten and then bakes. And, because it is so moist it keeps for days, but it won't last.

Pizzookie

This recipe is so much fun. We make them in pans big enough for two and it makes a great couples dessert. However, my kids make this all of the time. I make cookie dough and make half into cookies and save the other half in the fridge for pizzookie. If you have all of the ingredients on hand, it is a great anytime snack.

ingredients:

1 batch of your favorite Cookie Dough

Canned Whipped Cream

Good quality Vanilla Ice Cream

Chocolate syrup or sundae topping

Caramel or Butterscotch sundae topping

Preheat oven to 350 degrees

KIM'S NOTES:

7" pie pans or tart pans are what I usually use but smaller pans work great as an individual dessert. Don't be ashamed to use store-bought cookie dough. I do it all the time!

Kim's **easy steps**

1 Place room temperature cookie dough in a 7" pie plate (a tart pan or low edged cake pan would also work) and spread evenly around in pan. Dough should be about ½" thick (this would be enough dough to make 4 to 6 regular cookies).

2 Place pans on a cookie sheet and put them in the oven. Bake for 12 to 15 minutes until cookies look done, not too brown but starting to brown around the edges and have a little color.

3 Remove from oven and place pie pan on a larger plate. Working quickly, put a good sized scoop of ice cream in middle of cookie, put whipped cream around the outer edge of the cookie, then drizzle chocolate and caramel over the top.

4 Grab 2 forks or spoons and quickly share with a friend!

5 This dessert works great with chocolate chip cookie dough, white chocolate macadamia nut cookies (skip the chocolate syrup and double up on the caramel), peanut butter cookies (try this with caramel ice cream), or chocolate chocolate chip cookie dough (omit the caramel and sprinkle with mini chocolate chips). The sky is the limit. Have fun with this one — everyone else will!

desserts

Ingredients:

The Crust

2 cups Graham Cracker Crumbs (about 1½ packages crushed)

1 stick (8 Tbsp.) Butter, melted

½ cup granulated Sugar

1 tsp. ground Cinnamon

The Filling

12 oz. Cream Cheese, room temperature

1 cup Powdered Sugar, sifted

2 envelopes Dream Whip, prepared according to package directions

The Topping

2 21-oz. cans of best quality Cherry Pie Filling

This dessert has been a Christmas tradition in my husband's family for years. Now it has become one in our family, but I have to make two pans of it; one pan for my husband and one for the rest of us to share. It's like a fluffy cheesecake and best yet, there's no baking involved.

Kim's **easy steps**

Crust

1 In a medium bowl, combine all ingredients well and press into the bottom of a 9" x 13" pan.

Filling

2 Whip cream cheese and powdered sugar together with a hand mixer or with a wooden spoon until fluffy and well combined. Gently fold prepared Dream Whip into cream cheese mixture until well combined.

Spread filling on top of graham cracker crust. Smooth top and level as much as possible

Topping

3 Spoon cherry pie filling on top of cream cheese mixture and carefully spread cherries and sauce evenly over pie.

4 Cover pan with plastic wrap or foil and refrigerate for at least 3 hours, but it's even better if left overnight.

KIM'S NOTES:

Kim's Notes: This dessert is yummy with raspberry or blackberry pie filling too. Be adventurous!

A SPECIAL THANKS

There are so many people I want to thank for making this possible. This dream of mine could never have come true without the help and support of all of these people! First, my mom, Glenna Pizza, thank you for being the best kitchen assistant possible and for teaching me in your kitchen when I was young. I know now that it takes twice as long to accomplish something with the help of little ones.

Thanks to the gang at Orson Gygi, especially Brad and Mindy McDonald. Your facilities are wonderful and you made us feel like family from the very first shoot day.

Thanks to Steve Smith, my photographer. This book would not have been the same without your eye, your vision and your amazing talent. We make a great team. Sorry about the long days!

Thanks to Sara, Dick, Cheryl and Anne at Thomas Arts for bringing my layout to life and getting everything put together.

Thanks to Rick Larsen for lighting the fire in me to create this book. Also, thanks for introducing me to Operation Kids and for letting me be a small part of an amazing organization.

To Rick Evans, thank you for sharing your ideas and vision.

Thanks to Scott and Lesli Rice (my sister) for sharing your beautiful yard with me for the grilling recipes (and to Mike for being the official taster).

To Chuck and Gwen Warren (my in-laws), thank you for your support and encouragement from the very beginning of this project.

But most of all to my family, Annie, Katie, Charlie, and Parker for allowing me the time to follow this dream and for being such great helpers and tasting guinea pigs. To Natalie, for finding Steve, for being a great friend and for making my life a whole lot easier. I love you guys!

Finally, to my husband and sweetheart, Chuck. Thank you for encouraging me to get this done and for making it all happen. But most of all, thank you for always believing in me. I love you.

Alphabetical Index of Recipes